CW01510570

About this Learning Guide

Shmoop Will Make You a Better Lover*
*of Literature, History, Poetry, Life...

Our lively learning guides are written by experts and educators who want to show your brain a good time. Shmoop writers come primarily from Ph.D. programs at top universities, including Stanford, Harvard, and UC Berkeley.

Want more Shmoop? We cover literature, poetry, bestsellers, music, US history, civics, biographies (and the list keeps growing). Drop by our website to see the latest.

www.shmoop.com

©2010 Shmoop University, Inc. All Rights Reserved.
Talk to the Labradoodle... She's in Charge.

Table of Contents

Introduction

In a Nutshell

Anton Chekhov was a Russian writer famous for his short stories and plays. The *Cherry Orchard* was his last play, produced by the famous Moscow Art Theatre shortly before his death in 1904.

You may have heard that Chekhov was a doctor. He started writing to support himself during medical school, and you can see the bedside manner in his writing. He's a man who has seen a lot, and thinks of people with a mixture of affection and ridicule. You can certainly see this side of him in *The Cherry Orchard*, which depicts an aristocratic Russian family that loses their ancestral estate because they can't pay the mortgage.

Many consider *The Cherry Orchard* Chekhov's greatest play. It is a beautiful example of Chekhovian style: the mixture of comedy and tragedy, a form that avoids melodrama by setting the most exciting events offstage, and the detailed characterization that makes Chekhov an actor's dream.

Why Should I Care?

Imagine there is a beautiful park in your neighborhood. It's owned by one family and walled off from everyone else. But the family is almost never there; the park decays because they can't pay for its upkeep. Should the rest of the community be able to make use of that space?

Now think of the most beloved place in your hometown: a field, a patch of woods, a city block, the family home. You played there. You had your first kiss there. A million moments that make you *you* happened there. Fast-forward a few decades and someone wants to take this spot away from you. Obliterate it. Maybe turn it into a parking lot or a hotel. No one will ever know that this special place was there but you, and once you die, that's it. Would you fight for it?

These two scenarios play into *The Cherry Orchard*. This play is about the relentless march of time and the way people handle change. Some profit by it. Some go kicking and screaming. And others are left behind.

Summary

Book Summary

Act I opens with the businessman Lopakhin and maid Dunyasha waiting for the owners of the Ranevskaya estate: the mistress of the house, Lubov Ranevskaya, her brother Gaev, and daughter Anya. They finally arrive, in the middle of the night, with an assortment of others: the governess Charlotta, the manservant Yasha, a friend named Simeon-Pischik, and other

servants. Varya, Lubov's adopted daughter, is there too.

Tearful reunions and a general catching-up ensue. Those who stayed home report on the orchard, and those who left report on Paris. The important news items are these: Lopakhin *still* hasn't proposed to Varya; Lubov lost all her money supporting a scamp; the cherry orchard will definitely be sold to pay their debts; and the elderly servant Fiers is still alive.

Lopakhin has an idea to save their house. He's attached to it because he grew up there, the son of a serf (a peasant working on the land). Lopakhin proposes clearing the land to lease it for summer homes. Neither Lubov nor Gaev can stomach the idea. Just before everyone goes to bed, the student Trofimov enters. He was the tutor to Lubov's deceased young son, and the sight of his face makes her cry for her dead child.

In Act II, we're at a picnic in the cherry orchard. Some weeks have passed. The aristocrats arrive with Lopakhin, who is still hatching plans to save the estate. Lubov knows they need to do something, but to her the idea of summer homes is bourgeois and distasteful. Trofimov enters with Anya and Varya. Pet subjects come up: Varya's engagement; Trofimov's eternal student status; telegrams from Lubov's ne'er-do-well Parisian lover; and the orchard, again and again. A homeless man enters the scene, drunk and singing. He asks for money and Lubov gives him a gold piece, an oversized donation she immediately regrets upon his exit.

Everyone leaves, and finally Trofimov and Anya are left alone. Under his influence, she's come to see the orchard differently. It's no longer the magical center of her childhood, but a symbol of the injustice her family afflicted on others.

Act III is set in August, back at the family estate. Lubov is throwing a party. There are a number of little arguments and discussions. But the main event is the arrival of Lopakhin. He and Gaev have come from the auction of the cherry orchard. Lubov's been on pins and needles waiting to hear what happened. What happened is…Lopakhin bought the estate. The former son of a serf who worked on the estate now owns it. Lubov is crushed, but Anya gently tells her to move on.

Act IV takes place in October, outside the estate. Everyone is moving out, and Lopakhin, no master of sensitivity, offers champagne. Each character says good-bye to the house in his or her way. Anya and Trofimov are excited about the future. Lubov and Gaev are distraught, but trying to keep it together. Lubov is concerned about the elderly servant Fiers: have they taken him to the hospital? Yes, says Anya, he's taken care of. And one last thing: will Lopakhin finally propose to Varya? He won't. Everyone leaves, and after a moment, Fiers enters the stage. He has been forgotten. He lies down and grows quiet.

Act 1

- The businessman Lopakhin and young maid Dunyasha are in the nursery at Lubov Ranevskaya's house. They were waiting anxiously for Lubov to arrive from the train, but Lopakhin has fallen asleep.
- When he wakes up, he reminisces about Lubov showing him kindness as a little boy, though he was just a peasant. He's a rich man now.

- The clerk Epikhodov enters and gives a weather report: frost, though the cherry trees are in bloom. When he leaves, Dunyasha confesses to Lopakhin that the clerk has proposed to her. But he's accident-prone and has squeaky boots, so she's not sure she's into it.
- Two carriages drive up to the house. The old servant Fiers walks across the stage to meet the mistress of the house, Lubov. He mumbles to himself.
- Everyone enters! Lubov, her daughters Anya and Varya, her brother Gaev, the magician Charlotta, Simeon-Pischik, and a couple of servants.
- Lubov recognizes the nursery where she grew up, and weeps.
- When Anya and Dunyasha are left alone, Dunyasha confides that Epikhodov has proposed. Anya is indifferent and exhausted.
- Varya enters with her keys. She's been left behind to take care of the house. Anya gives an account of living in Paris with Charlotta and Lubov. It was cold; her French was horrible; her mother is penniless.
- Anya asks Varya a question that will be repeated throughout the play: has Lopakhin proposed? No, says Varya, and she doubts he will. She wishes people would stop pushing it.
- The servant Yasha enters. He sexually harasses Dunyasha and she breaks a saucer.
- Anya and Varya talk about Trofimov. He was their little brother Grisha's tutor before his death – right after Lubov's husband's death.
- Fiers scolds Dunyasha for not having the coffee ready, then weeps with happiness that the mistress is back home. (Comedy and sentimentality are often butted up right next to each other in Chekhov.)
- The older generation reenters: Lubov with her brother Gaev. They are reminiscing, and as Lopakhin tries to contribute, Gaev embarrasses him.
- A little more small talk and Lopakhin comes out with it: the cherry orchard is going to be sold if they don't do something about it. He has a plan. They just need to divide the land into building lots for summer homes, rent them out, and make enough money to pay their debts.
- Ranevskaya and Gaev look at him blankly. They can't imagine selling this land where they grew up.
- Varya enters with two telegrams for Ranevskaya. They are from Paris. She rips them up without reading them.
- Totally ignoring Lopakhin's proposal for the cherry orchard, Gaev makes an ode to the bookcase.
- Lopakhin finally leaves. Pischik asks Lubov to loan him money, and Varya protests they haven't got it. More teasing about Varya marrying Lopakhin ensues.
- They're all about to go to bed. The sun is coming up outside, and Gaev and Lubov notice that the orchard is all white. Lubov imagines she sees her mother walking towards her.
- Trofimov enters. He was Grisha's tutor. At first Lubov doesn't recognize him; then she bursts into tears, thinking of her dead son. She's depressed at how old Trofimov looks.
- Before going to bed, Lubov agrees to loan Pischik money.
- Yasha won't see his mother, who's been waiting in the kitchen since yesterday. She's a peasant, and he's become almost a gentleman.
- Gaev proposes a few options for saving the orchard: Anya's marriage to a rich man, the intervention of a wealthy aunt, an inheritance. Varya wishes for the help of God.
- Part of the problem, says Gaev, is that Lubov is a little morally loose. Anya overhears this and scolds Gaev for slandering her mother.

- Both Anya and Varya agree Gaev should keep his trap shut more often. But he's in a state: he's figured out three courses of action to save the orchard. He will arrange a loan from somebody at the District Court; Lubov will sweet-talk Lopakhin; and Anya will try the rich aunt. Something's got to work out.
- All this planning soothes Anya. She's sure it will be OK.
- Fiers still regards Gaev as a child. He reprimands him for staying up late. Before Gaev goes to bed, he makes one last speech about treating peasants well – to the chagrin of Anya and Varya.
- Varya tells Anya that some vagrants started sleeping in the servant's quarters, relying on her to feed them. But Anya has fallen asleep.
- As Varya takes Anya to bed, Trofimov sees her for the first time in several years. He is moved.

Act 2

- Everyone's having a picnic outside.
- Charlotta is musing about her unconventional life. She doesn't know how old she is. Her parents were performers and, when they died, a German lady took her in. She became a governess. Now she's alone.
- Epikhodov plays on a guitar. He's trying to get Dunyasha's attention, but she's not having it. Her eye is on Yasha.
- When Epikhodov shows off a revolver, Charlotta decides she's had enough of these people. She takes off.
- Epikhodov is full of dissatisfaction, too. He feels wronged by fate. He'd like a private word with Dunyasha, but she sends him on an errand.
- Dunyasha intimates to Yasha what a lady she is, and that he better not treat her badly.
- He kisses her. Then tells her to behave. When Lubov approaches, Yasha asks Dunyasha to get lost. It would look bad for them to be seen together.
- Lubov enters with Gaev and Lopakhin. Lopakhin is on his pet subject: will they rent the cherry orchard for villas?
- Lubov and Gaev totally ignore him. Lubov seems to be in a bad mood. She drops her coins and blames herself for spending money on lunch when Varya is feeding the peasants peas. She also scolds her brother for eating so much, drinking so much, talking so much.
- Yasha is teasing Gaev, who can't stand it. It's either him or me, Gaev says. Lubov dismisses Yasha.
- Lopakhin informs them that a rich man from town plans to buy their estate. When Lubov counters that their aunt will loan them money – maybe ten thousand rubles – Lopakhin is beside himself. It's not going to be enough. They have to rent the cherry orchard out for vacation villas.
- But it's so vulgar! protests Lubov.
- Lopakhin threatens to leave, but Lubov apologizes. She feels she's led a sinful life, wasting money, marrying a good-for-nothing drunk. She thinks her son died as a punishment. After he died, she took up with another good-for-nothing, who fell ill and drained her emotionally and financially. He just sent her another telegram, which she tears

up.

- A Jewish band can be heard. Lubov wants to have them over.
- On the subject of entertainment, Lopakhin saw a play last night. Lubov says he should spend time looking at his own life instead of plays. And he should get married. To Varya.
- Lopakhin is noncommittal.
- Gaev has been offered a job in a bank. Fiers enters with Gaev's overcoat, scolding him.
- Fiers talks about the emancipation – he didn't agree with it. He stayed in service even after being freed.
- Anya and Varya enter with Trofimov. Lopakhin teases him for always being with the ladies. And still being a student.
- Trofimov has heard it before, but still gets riled.
- They make fun of him, but they enjoy hearing Trofimov's opinions. He believes in work and progress. He loathes the intellectuals who still treat their servants like animals.
- Lopakhin picks up on the thread, reflecting on how small and petty people are, when they should really be giants.
- Epikhodov enters with his guitar. Everyone's feeling pensive.
- Gaev can't help himself. He sees the sunset and delivers an ode to Nature. Anya and Varya hush him.
- Everyone is silent for a moment, then a distant sound like a breaking string is heard. It disturbs them.
- Soon after, a drunken vagrant enters, begging for money. Varya screams; Lubov gives him a gold piece. Varya can't believe Lubov gave him so much.
- When Lubov brings up marriage, Lopakhin makes some bad nun jokes in Varya's direction. Everyone exits, aside from Trofimov and Anya.
- They are relieved to be alone.
- Trofimov is annoyed that Varya keeps monitoring them. She's afraid they'll fall in love, he says. But they have higher things in mind.
- Anya is under his spell. He's made her see the cherry orchard totally differently. She doesn't love it like she used to.
- Of course she doesn't love it, says Trofimov. It's a symbol of slavery. Her ancestors owned serfs, whose souls haunt the trees. They have to escape the past.
- Anya will start with leaving the house. Trofimov is all for it.
- Epikhodov's guitar is heard, and Varya, calling for them.

Act 3

- It's a party at Lubov's house. The Jewish band from Act 2 is playing, people are dancing and playing pool, Pischik is talking nonsense to Trofimov.
- When Varya enters, Trofimov gives her the usual taunt: "Madame Lopakhin!"
- Pischik is trying to scrounge up money to pay interest. For a minute he freaks out, thinking he's lost what he already collected.
- Trofimov wryly observes that Pischik could move mountains with the energy he's spent finding money.
- Today is the day of the auction and Lubov is waiting anxiously for news.

- Meanwhile Charlotta is entertaining everyone with parlor tricks: cards, ventriloquism, and disappearing acts. Pischik is a little smitten.
- Trying to soothe her mother, Varya assures her that Gaev has bought the orchard.
- The topic of Varya's marriage to Lopakhin comes up again. She likes him, she admits, but she can't really propose to him herself.
- Yasha comes in laughing and tattling: Epikhodov has broken a billiard cue. Varya is miffed that Epikhodov, a worker, is acting like a guest.
- Lubov asks Trofimov not to tease Varya so much. Can't he see how unhappy she is?
- He's just getting back at her for hounding him and Anya. They are above love.
- Lubov says she must be beneath love. But really, all she can think about is the auction. She wants Trofimov to comfort her.
- She's got the wrong man. Trofimov tells her to look reality in the face.
- Lubov can't believe his lack of sympathy. He only thinks he knows what reality is because of his youth, because he hasn't seen the worst of life.
- A telegram falls out of Lubov's sleeve. It's from her lover in Paris, who is sick and begging her to return.
- She still loves this man, who has stolen everything from her? She's a fool, says Trofimov.
- This infuriates Lubov. She attacks Trofimov, calling him a virgin and a freak.
- Trofimov is horrified. He leaves the room, and promptly falls down the stairs.
- The dancing starts again. Lubov apologizes and dances with Trofimov.
- Fiers comes in, disapproving of the whole scene. He tells Yasha how, in the past, generals and barons came to their parties. Today it's post office clerks.
- Yasha replies that he's bored and wishes Fiers would kick the bucket.
- Lubov asks Fiers where he will go if the estate is sold. Wherever she tells him, he says.
- Yasha requests that Lubov take him back to Paris. The people here are too uneducated for him.
- Dunyasha enters, trying to get Yasha's attention. She's been flirting with the post office clerk. Epikhodov still has a thing for her, but she won't give him any time.
- Varya scolds Epikhodov for breaking the cue. When she threatens to hit him with a stick, she catches Lopakhin instead.
- He's back from the auction. With Gaev, who's wiping tears from his eyes.
- The orchard has been sold. To Lopakhin.
- Lubov is stunned. Varya takes off her key ring and throws it down.
- Lopakhin tells the story of the auction. A rich man was making bids, and Lopakhin topped him. The place where his father and grandfather were serfs now belongs to him.
- Lopakhin asks for the musicians to play. Lubov weeps bitterly.
- Anya comes in, imploring her mother to stop crying and to move on.

Act 4

- The house has been stripped. Piles of suitcases are waiting outside.
- Lubov and Gaev have just said goodbye to the peasants living on their estate. Lubov gave them all her money.
- Lopakhin excitedly offers everyone champagne. No one will drink it, except Yasha.

- The train leaves in 47 minutes, Lopakhin reminds everyone.
- Lopakhin and Trofimov have a little chat. There is sympathy between the two of them, though they tease each other. Lopakhin offers Trofimov money, which he declines.
- The sounds of chopping wood can be heard. Can't they wait till Lubov is gone, asks Anya?
- One item to be resolved: Fiers. Anya inquires what has become of him. Was he sent to the doctor? Yasha replies irritably that he dealt with it this morning.
- Yasha again refuses his mother and rejects Dunyasha. He's happy to be getting out of here.
- Lubov enters with Anya, who's also happy to be leaving and starting a new life. She plans to further her education, work, and read a lot of books.
- Gaev is looking on the bright side. At least it's all been resolved, and he's got a new job.
- Charlotta's singing. She makes a baby out of a bundle, then throws it away. She doesn't know what's happening to her. Lopakhin promises to figure something out.
- Pischik enters and shocks everyone by paying back the money he's borrowed. Some Englishmen leased his land for its white clay. He hadn't realized the family is leaving today, but accepts their departure.
- Lubov is worried about Fiers. Anya assures her that Yasha took care of him.
- Lubov is also worried about Varya. She has a private moment with Lopakhin. Seriously, won't he propose to her?
- Sure, okay, now's the time, he agrees. Varya is sent for.
- They are alone. A couple pleasantries, some awkward pauses. Lopakhin doesn't do it. Varya weeps.
- Everyone gets ready to go. Anya is excited. Gaev starts making a speech…and stops. They'll see each other in the spring. Lopakhin starts locking up.
- Everyone exits, leaving Lubov and Gaev alone. They sob.
- After a moment, they leave too. The stage is empty. More sounds of locking doors, and the sounds of trees being chopped.
- Fiers enters. He's sick. They've forgotten him. He sits on a sofa, worrying about what coat Gaev has on. He lies down, and stops moving.
- Again, the sound of a string breaking is heard. Then just the sound of an axe falling on trees.

Themes

Theme of Society and Class

Class instability is the driving circumstance in *The Cherry Orchard.* Chekhov portrays Russia after in the freeing of the serfs, in a moment of flux. While the society used to be well-stratified, now everything's all mixed up. There are servants who want to stay servants, like 87-year-old Fiers. There are servants who pretend to be ladies and gentlemen, like Dunyasha and Yasha. There are former peasants who are rich and getting richer, like Lopakhin. And the aristocrats on their way nowhere but down.

Questions About Society and Class

1. Why does Gaev have such a problem with Yasha and Lopakhin?
2. Does Trofimov's student status place him outside of the social hierarchy?
3. Why do the servants (Yasha, Dunyasha, Epikhodov) constantly pose as higher class than they are?

Chew on Society and Class

As Lubov's servants, Fiers and Yasha embody the change in social attitudes in turn-of-century Russia.

Trofimov's monologues make explicit the ideas of social change embedded in the play.

Theme of Memory and the Past

Because *The Cherry Orchard* depicts a changing society, the characters spend a lot of time thinking about how *now* compares to *then*. How characters relate to the past determines their investment in the play's major question: will the cherry orchard be saved? As a symbol of the past of the Russian empire, the orchard evokes longing, regret, or disgust – sometimes a combination of all three. Despite the painful resistance of most characters, in the end, a cord to the past is snipped. The cherry orchard is sold, the house is shuttered, and the old servant is left to die.

Questions About Memory and the Past

1. Who do you think is the most sentimental and nostalgic character in the play?
2. Varya is Lubov's adopted daughter. What is her relationship to the past and how does it differ from Anya's?
3. Is there any character in the play unmoved by memories of the past?

Chew on Memory and the Past

Chekhov uses Fiers's senility as a tool of remembrance in the play.

How characters respond to the loss of the cherry orchard defines their dependence on, or freedom from, the weight of the past.

Theme of Love

For a play about social change, *The Cherry Orchard* abounds in love. There are love triangles. There is unrequited love. There's physical love. There's spiritual love. Maternal love. Platonic love. Love between master and servant. There's even requited love! Chekhov just couldn't write a play about human beings without showing them in love of all kinds and making decisions, good and bad, inspired by love.

Questions About Love

1. Why doesn't Lopakhin propose to Varya?
2. Is Trofimov really "above love," as he claims?
3. How does Lubov's attitude toward love relate to her attitude toward money?
4. What will happen to Dunyasha now that Yasha's returning to Paris? Will she decide to marry Epikhodov?

Chew on Love

As Lubov's daughter, Anya offers the love needed to humanize Trofimov's ideals.

Lubov's devotion to love provides a counterpoint to Trofimov's purely sociological perspective.

Theme of Mortality

There's a good amount of death in *The Cherry Orchard*. It is mentioned over and over. The memory of a dead son and husband haunt the main character, Lubov. The clown threatens to kill himself. Departing family describe the house as "at the end of its life." And though Chekhov isn't explicit about it, we're pretty sure we witness the death of Fiers, the loyal old servant. Just like the shifting social landscape, death is an inevitable part of life.

Questions About Mortality

1. Do you believe Epikhodov might kill himself?
2. How do the deaths of her husband and son affect Lubov's relationship to the orchard?
3. Do you think Fiers dies at the end of the play? If so, why?

Chew on Mortality

Death is a shadow that drives Lubov to love.

The Cherry Orchard is about the death of a way of life.

Theme of Home

The Cherry Orchard begins with a homecoming. The main character Lubov believes that, in returning home, she can restore her life to a state of innocence. Ever heard that saying, "You can never go home again?" Lubov learns the hard way. Home has become a bittersweet mixture of happy and sad memories, worry, and conflict. It's under siege by economic forces and social change. *The Cherry Orchard* begins with a homecoming, but ends – just six months later – with an eviction.

Questions About Home

1. How does each character define home?
2. What does Lubov come home looking for?
3. What do you make of Charlotta's homelessness?
4. Why is Varya left behind to look after the house?

Chew on Home

Trofimov's home is in his head, and he invites Anya to live there.

Abandoned to the estate and, at the end of the play, a new family, Varya is just as orphaned as Charlotta.

Theme of Time

"Time," says Lopakhin the businessman, "does go" (1.83). Profound? Not so much – but a strong undercurrent in *The Cherry Orchard*. Characters are acutely aware of the passage of time. The industrious characters (Varya and Lopakhin) check their watches regularly, reflecting the industrial age's increasingly strict relationship to time. The more old-fashioned, leisurely characters lament their age. They comment on the weather as it changes from May to October. Some of them even celebrate the 100th birthday of a bookcase.

Questions About Time

1. Chekhov is pretty specific about when the events take place: from May to October. Why?
2. Can you divide the characters into camps – pro-orchard or anti-orchard – depending on their age?
3. Trofimov says that man is evolving over time. Is that thesis carried out by the play?

Chew on Time

Trofimov's virginity represents his immaturity.

Lopakhin and Varya share a punctuality, related to their work ethic, that distinguishes them from the other characters.

Theme of Wealth

When it comes to money, nobody's neutral in *The Cherry Orchard*. Characters are begging for it, borrowing it, planning to make more of it, or proudly declaring their independence from it. An aristocratic family, impractical and naïve, continues to spend as they might have a hundred years ago. They've never worked for money and can't begin now. Meanwhile, the son of a serf draws on his resources – mainly, a willingness to work hard – to build a fortune.

Questions About Wealth

1. Is Trofimov really indifferent to his poverty?
2. How important is money to Lopakhin?
3. Why does Lubov throw money away?

Chew on Wealth

With his industrious collection of money, Pischik is a comic foil for Lubov.

Lopakhin ceaselessly pursues wealth to bury his father's memory.

Theme of Contrasting Regions

Many of the characters in *The Cherry Orchard* pinball between "there" and "here" in futile efforts of escape. Lubov runs from her unhappy relationship in Paris, believing that Russia will offer her stability and comfort. When she realizes that home in Russia is just as unstable as abroad, maybe more so, she runs back. Her servant Yasha shares her desire to leave, but he only wants a one-way ticket – from his peasant background to the good and lazy life in Paris.

Questions About Contrasting Regions

1. Why does Chekhov choose Paris as the setting for Lubov's other life?
2. Of all the characters, Yasha seems to be the most certain that he wants to return to Paris. Why?
3. Why does Lubov return to Russia in the first place?

Chew on Contrasting Regions

At the beginning of the play, Anya finds Paris inhospitable and Russia the only place to be. Trofimov expands her field of vision, igniting in her a desire for travel.

Dunyasha seeks Yasha's attention hoping that his sheen of worldliness will rub off on her.

Society and Class Quotes

LOPAKHIN. My father was a peasant, it's true, but here I am in a white waistcoat and yellow shoes ... a pearl out of an oyster. I'm rich now, with lots of money, but just think about it and examine me, and you'll find I'm still a peasant down to the marrow of my bones. (1.5)

Thought: Lopakhin knows himself well. He admires and desires upper-class life, but doesn't believe he can truly inhabit it.

LOPAKHIN. You're too sensitive, Dunyasha. You dress just like a lady, and you do your hair like one too. You oughtn't. You should know your place. (1.9)

Thought: Everyone's always telling Dunyasha to know her place. Yet Lopakhin is the quintessential striver, escaping from his lower-class roots to eventually buy the orchard.

GAEV. It smells of patchouli here. (1.86)

Thought: Gaev is very sensitive to smells and likes to comment on working-class ones to put people in their place, particularly Lopakhin and Yasha.

LOPAKHIN. Up to now in the villages there were only the gentry and the labourers, and now the people who live in villas have arrived. All towns now, even small ones, are surrounded by villas. And it's safe to say that in twenty years' time the villa resident will be all over the place. At present he sits on his balcony and drinks tea, but it may well come to pass that he'll begin to cultivate his patch of land, and then your cherry orchard will be happy, rich, splendid. (1.124)

Thought: Lopakhin just really doesn't know how to speak their language. Does he think that Lubov and Gaev will be enamored of the image of hundreds of burghers setting up house on their land?

VARYA. [To YASHA] Your mother's come from the village; she's been sitting in the servants' room since yesterday, and wants to see you. ...

YASHA. Bless the woman!

VARYA. Shameless man. (1.192-194)

Thought: Though he is a servant, Yasha wants to be a man of leisure. He won't acknowledge his mother, who reminds him of his peasant past.

GAEV. The peasants don't love me for nothing, I assure you. We've got to learn to know the peasants! (1.214)

Thought: Do the peasants really love Gaev? Does he have anything to do with them? The only interactions we see are the encounter with the vagrant – which Gaev handles with total distaste – and a farewell speech at the top of Act 4.

VARYA. In the old servants' part of the house, as you know, only the old people live--little old Efim and Polya and Evstigney, and Karp as well. They started letting some tramps or other spend the night there--I said nothing. Then I heard that they were saying that I had ordered them to be fed on peas and nothing else; from meanness, you see. ... And it was all Evstigney's doing. (1.220)

Thought: Because Varya has practical dealings with the peasants, she bears the brunt of class tensions. She can't afford to be as magnanimous as Lubov.

DUNYASHA. I went into service when I was quite a little girl, and now I'm not used to common life, and my hands are white, white as a lady's. I'm so tender and so delicate now; respectable and afraid of everything. (2.18)

Thought: Dunyasha is doing what our grandmother called "putting on airs." She tries to attract the newly cosmopolitan Yasha by claiming to be a lady.

YASHA. Of course, every girl must respect herself; there's nothing I dislike more than a badly behaved girl. (2.19)

Thought: When it comes to "knowing one's place," Yasha is a hypocrite. He believes he can act like a gentleman, while counseling Dunyasha to remember to be subservient.

LOPAKHIN. I've never learned anything, my handwriting is bad, I write so that I'm quite ashamed before people, like a pig! (2.64)

Thought: Lopakhin is equally honest about his background, whether he's with servants or aristocrats.

VARYA. Why is Epikhodov here? Who said he could play billiards? I don't understand these people. (3.51)

Thought: Varya is more conservative and hierarchical than the generation above her. Gaev and Lubov don't seem to care that the workers are enjoying themselves at the party, but Varya can't stand it.

Memory and the Past Quotes

LOPAKHIN. Lubov Andreyevna, as I remember her now, was still young, and very thin, and she took me to the washstand here in this very room, the nursery. (1.5)

Thought: Lopakhin may be a businessman, but he is almost as sentimental as Lubov. His devotion to her stems from this one memory, when she comforted him as a little boy.

LUBOV. My dear nursery, oh, you beautiful room. ... I used to sleep here when I was a baby. (1.26)

Thought: For Lubov, each present moment in the house – each encounter with a room or an object – reminds her of the past. It's almost as though the house is haunted.

ANYA. [Thoughtfully] Father died six years ago, and a month later my brother Grisha was drowned in the river--such a dear little boy of seven! Mother couldn't bear it; she went away, away, without looking round. (1.75)

Thought: Lubov once fled her home in grief, fearing to encounter memories of her husband and son. Now she fears losing those memories with the loss of the estate.

GAEV. Once upon a time you and I used both to sleep in this room, and now I'm fifty-one; it does seem strange. (1.82)

Thought: Gaev and Lubov feed each other's obsessions with the past.

FIERS. In the old days, forty or fifty years back, they dried the cherries, soaked them and pickled them, and made jam of them…and then we'd send the dried cherries off in carts to Moscow and Kharkov. And money! And the dried cherries were soft, juicy, sweet, and nicely scented. ... They knew the way. (1.115)

Thought: Fiers represents the past that is perishing. He remembers the vitality of the cherry orchard. But he can't remember the recipe for the jam – the practical knowledge that made the orchard sustainable.

LUBOV. [Looks out into the garden] Oh, my childhood, days of my innocence! In this nursery I used to sleep; I used to look out from here into the orchard. Happiness used to wake with me every morning, and then it was just as it is now; nothing has changed. (1.162)

Thought: Wake up, Lubov! Everything has changed. Serfs have been freed, the trees don't yield fruit, the estate is about to be sold.

LUBOV. Look, there's my dead mother going in the orchard ...dressed in white! [Laughs from joy] That's she. (1.164)

Thought: Just when we want to strangle Lubov for refusing to face reality, Chekhov gives her a heartbreaking moment like this.

TROFIMOV. For it's so clear that in order to begin to live in the present we must first redeem the past, and that can only be done by suffering, by strenuous, uninterrupted labour. Understand that, Anya. (2.149)

Thought: Trofimov's view of the past is completely contrary to Lubov's. Life on the estate was not beautiful and idyllic – it was unjust.

LUBOV. To look at the walls and the windows for the last time. ...My dead mother used to like to walk about this room. (4.129)

Thought: Lubov and Gaev can't stop recounting memories as they prepare to leave the house.

GAEV. I remember, when I was six years old, on Trinity Sunday, I sat at this window and looked and saw my father going to church. i(4.106)

Thought: Lubov remembers her mother, Gaev remembers his father. Perhaps they both see themselves in these images of the past.

Love Quotes

DUNYASHA. I don't know what to do about it. He's a nice young man, but every now and again, when he begins talking, you can't understand a word he's saying. I think I like him. He's madly in love with me. He's an unlucky man; every day something happens. (1.19)

Thought: At the beginning of the play, Dunyasha entertains the idea of attaching herself to Epikhodov. Under the sexual influence of Yasha, however, she quickly learns to ignore him.

LOPAKHIN. There they are, right enough. Let's go and meet them. Will she know me? We haven't seen each other for five years. (1.21)

Thought: Lopakhin seems to have a crush on Lubov. We can imagine him dreaming up scenarios in which he marries her to save the orchard.

DUNYASHA. The clerk, Epikhodov, proposed to me after Easter.

ANYA. Always the same. (1.34-35)

Thought: Anya is bored by Dunyasha's narcissism. She largely stays out of the conversations about who should be engaged to whom, even before she reconnects with Mr. "Above-Love."

LOPAKHIN. My father was the serf of your grandfather and your own father, but you--you more than anybody else--did so much for me once upon a time that I've forgotten everything and love you as if you belonged to my family ... and even more. (1.101)

Thought: Is it possible that some of Lopakhin's affection for Lubov is actually a Fiers-like servant/master devotion?

VARYA. I think that it will all come to nothing. He's a busy man. I'm not his affair ... he pays no attention to me. Bless the man, I don't want to see him. ... But everybody talks about our marriage, everybody congratulates me, and there's nothing in it at all, it's all like a dream. (1.60)

Thought: It's hard to know from the text whether Varya really loves Lopakhin. Her desire to marry him could spring solely from a desire for security and companionship.

VARYA. My darling's come back, my pretty one's come back! ...I go about all day, looking after the house, and I think all the time, if only you could marry a rich man, then I'd be happy and would go away somewhere by myself, then to Kiev ... to Moscow, and so on, from one holy place to another. I'd tramp and tramp. That would be splendid! (1.62)

Thought: As caretaker of the estate, Varya doesn't think of marriage in terms of love. Anya's marriage to a rich man would be a suitable solution for a difficult problem – and would allow Varya to do what she wants.

TROFIMOV. Varya's afraid we may fall in love with each other and won't get away from us for days on end. Her narrow mind won't allow her to understand that we are above love. (2.145)

Thought: As usual, Trofimov lacks compassion for those around him. His idealistic, militant perspective keeps him from seeing the need that motivates others – in Varya's case, her loneliness.

VARYA. I can't propose to him myself, little mother. People have been talking about him to me for two years now, but he either says nothing, or jokes about it. I understand. He's getting rich, he's busy, he can't bother about me. (3.47)

Thought: Varya seems to be the character who is most trapped by external circumstances. She's stuck taking care of the estate. Why is it that Lopakhin is the only option for her marriage?

TROFIMOV As if I'd ever given her grounds to believe I'd stoop to such vulgarity! We are above love.

LUBOV. Then I suppose I must be beneath love. (4.53-54)

Thought: Trofimov claims that love is a waste of time. Lubov regards love as an overpowering force. Does Chekhov seem to believe one or the other?

LUBOV. I love him, that's plain, I love him, I love him. ... That love is a stone round my neck; I'm going with it to the bottom, but I love that stone and can't live without it. (4.60)

Thought: Lubov goes from tearing up her lover's telegrams to planning to return to him. What happened? Did she love him the whole time? Or is he something to run to when the cherry orchard is lost?

Mortality Quotes

ANYA. [Thoughtfully] Father died six years ago, and a month later my brother Grisha was drowned in the river--such a dear little boy of seven! (1.75)

Thought: From the beginning of the play, death is on the characters' minds. They remember the deaths of Lubov's husband and Grisha, and regularly comment on Fiers's closeness to death.

FIERS. [Joyfully] The mistress is home again. I've lived to see her! Don't care if I die now. ... [Weeps with joy.] (1.80)

Thought: Like Anfisa in *Three Sisters*, Fiers is the dedicated old servant who eventually outlives his usefulness. He becomes a burden, a problem to be dealt with, even as he seeks to serve.

LUBOV. Thank you, Fiers. Thank you, dear old man. I'm so glad you're still with us. (1.96)

Thought: Fiers is a link to times gone by. The fact that he's still alive, wearing his livery, scolding Gaev as if he were a child, allows Lubov to hang on to the past.

GAEV. Nurse has died in your absence.

LUBOV. [Sits and drinks coffee] Yes, bless her soul. I heard by letter. (1.103-104)

Thought: Gaev catches Lubov up on who's dead and who's moved.

VARYA. *He's been mumbling away for three years. We're used to that.*

YASHA. *Senile decay. (1.142)*

Thought: Trofimov isn't a very compassionate guy, but Yasha takes the cake. He has nothing but contempt for the ailing Fiers.

TROFIMOV. *Peter Trofimov, once the tutor of your Grisha. ... Have I changed so much? (1.170)*

[LUBOV ANDREYEVNA embraces him and cries softly.]

Thought: Lubov hasn't seen Trofimov since her son's death. She associates him with the tragedy. Perhaps she hadn't expected to see such a vivid reminder of Grisha.

TROFIMOV. *Who knows? And what does it mean--you'll die? Perhaps a man has a hundred senses, and when he dies only the five known to us are destroyed and the remaining ninety-five are left alive. (2.102)*

Thought: Trofimov presents an alternate version of life after death. His ideas are inspired by science, not religion.

GAEV *[Not loudly, as if declaiming]* O Nature, *thou art wonderful, thou shinest with eternal radiance! Oh, beautiful and indifferent one, thou whom we call mother, thou containest in thyself existence and death, thou livest and destroyest. (2.111)*

Thought: Again, Gaev gives a ridiculous, inappropriate speech that nonetheless provides context. Despite Gaev's personal attachment to the cherry orchard and the estate, in this moment he recognizes his own minuteness. In the vastness of time and nature, his desires don't matter.

YASHA. *I'm tired of you, grandfather. [Yawns] If you'd only hurry up and kick the bucket. (3.76)*

Thought: Fiers is hardworking and subservient, while Yasha is lazy and impertinent. Perhaps Yasha wants Fiers out of the way so he doesn't suffer by comparison.

EPIKHODOV. *The aged Fiers, in my conclusive opinion, isn't worth mending; his forefathers had better have him. I only envy him. (4.40)*

Thought: Epikhodov is also somewhat of a lazy, impertinent employee. Like Yasha, he probably wouldn't mind if the faithful Fiers died. But in the face of Dunyasha's rejection, he's become casually suicidal himself.

FIERS. *[Lying down]* *I'll lie down. ...You've no strength left in you, nothing left at all. ... Oh, you ...bungler! [He lies without moving.] (1.134)*

Thought: Chekhov doesn't come out and say it, but it looks like Fiers has died. Lubov and Gaev, despite their affection for Fiers, have departed without leaving provision for him.

Home Quotes

VARYA. Well, you've come, glory be to God. Home again. [Caressing her] My darling is home again! My pretty one is back again! (1.43)

Thought: For Varya, the return of Lubov and Anya changes the definition of home. The house becomes not just a responsibility and headache, but a source of love and comfort.

ANYA. We went to Paris; it's cold there and snowing. I talk French perfectly horribly. My mother lives on the fifth floor. I go to her, and find her there with various Frenchmen, women, an old abbé with a book, and everything in tobacco smoke and with no comfort at all. I suddenly became very sorry for mother--so sorry that I took her head in my arms and hugged her and wouldn't let her go. Then mother started hugging me and crying. (1.48)

Thought: When Anya sees her mother far from home, among strangers, she plays the role of comforter. In *The Cherry Orchard*, the older generation often needs to be cared for.

ANYA. How's business? Has the interest been paid?

VARYA. Not much chance of that.

ANYA. Oh God, oh God ...

VARYA. The place will be sold in August.

ANYA. O God. (1.52-56)

Thought: When she first arrives home, Anya is completely in line with her mother's point of view: the estate must be saved. Her opinion changes as the play goes on.

LUBOV. God knows I love my own country, I love it deeply; I couldn't look out of the railway carriage, I cried so much. (1.96)

Thought: Lubov is immensely moved and relieved to return home. Does she intend to stay?

LOPAKHIN. As you already know, your cherry orchard is to be sold to pay your debts, and the sale is fixed for August 22. (1.107)

Thought: Lopakhin spends a good deal of the play strategizing about how to save the estate. He has a sentimental attachment too, but Gaev and Lubov refuse to acknowledge it.

GAEV. This orchard is mentioned in the "Encyclopaedic Dictionary." (1.113)

Thought: Gaev's identity has been defined by his background, represented by the famous cherry orchard. As the play ends, he attempts to redefine himself as a businessman

ANYA. What have you done to me, Peter? I don't love the cherry orchard as I used to. I loved it so tenderly, I thought there was no better place in the world than our orchard. (2.148)

Thought: Influenced by Trofimov's progressive ideals, Anya has loosened the nostalgic grip of her childhood home. She's growing up, distinguishing herself from her mother.

LUBOV. I was born here, my father and mother lived here, my grandfather too, I love this house. I couldn't understand my life without that cherry orchard, and if it really must be sold, sell me with it! ... My son was drowned here. (3.56)

Thought: Lubov is excitable. She exaggerates. But if we really believe that the orchard defines her, the loss of it is much more tragic.

LUBOV. I'll sit here one more minute. It's as if I'd never really noticed what the walls and ceilings of this house were like, and now I look at them greedily, with such tender love. (4.105)

Thought: For all her life, Lubov looked at her home as a loved one, so familiar, accepted and dismissed. As she looks for the last time, she tries to consume the house with her eyes, to take it with her.

LUBOV. My dear, my gentle, beautiful orchard! My life, my youth, my happiness, good-bye! Good-bye! (4.126)

Thought: Can a person's identity truly be linked to a place? Will Lubov really cease to be Lubov when the cherry orchard is cut down?

Time Quotes

LOPAKHIN. *The train's arrived, thank God. What's the time?*

DUNYASHA. *It will soon be two. [Blows out candle] It is light already. (1.1-2)*

Thought: The first line of the play gives us a lot of information. We don't know who Lopakhin is, but we know that a train has brought something he desperately wants. And that he's anxious about time. The situation of the play – saving the orchard before time runs out – is hinted at very early.

LOPAKHIN. *Yes, time does go.*

GAEV. *Who does?*

LOPAKHIN. *I said that time does go. (1.83-85)*

Thought: Lopakhin's not really trying to philosophize; he's just making conversation until he gets up the nerve to talk about the cherry orchard.

VARYA. *[To LOPAKHIN and PISCHIN] Well, sirs, it's getting on for three, quite time you went.*

LUBOV. *[Laughs] You're just the same as ever, Varya. (1.93-94)*

Thought: Varya is the house's rule-keeper. She has a pragmatic view of time that seems well-matched with Lopakhin's.

LOPAKHIN. *[Looks at his watch] I'm going away at once, I haven't much time ... but I'll tell you all about it in two or three words. (1.107)*

Thought: This is how Lopakhin introduces the idea of chopping down the orchard? By rushing through it in two or three words? Lopakhin's approach points up his frame of reference – so different from Lubov, who is leisurely drinking her coffee.

LOPAKHIN. *We shall see each other in three weeks. [Kisses LUBOV ANDREYEVNA'S hand] Now, good-bye. It's time to go. (1.148)*

Thought: As a representative of the modern, business-minded, time-obsessed world, Lopakhin constantly has to wrangle the lax, old-world Ranevskaya family.

GAEV. And do you know, Luba, how old this case is? A week ago I took out the bottom drawer; I looked and saw figures burnt out in it. That case was made exactly a hundred years ago. What do you think of that? What? We could celebrate its jubilee. It hasn't a soul of its own, but still, say what you will, it's a fine bookcase. (1.127)

Thought: Gaev's speech to the 100-year-old cabinet may be silly, but it reminds us of the history of the estate and how much has changed in the last century.

GAEV. I'm a man of the eighties. ... People don't praise those years much, but I can still say that I've suffered for my beliefs. (1.214)

Thought: Gaev admits his antiquity without embarrassment. There's almost a willful denial of progress in the things he says.

FIERS. I'm not well. At our balls some time back, generals and barons and admirals used to dance, and now we send for post-office clerks and the Station-master, and even they come as a favour. I'm very weak. (3.75)

Thought: Even more than Lubov and Gaev, Fiers regrets how things have changed over time. By juxtaposing his observations of their social decline with comments about Fiers's health, Chekhov seems to hint that the two are (at least symbolically) connected.

Ladies and gentlemen, please remember that it's only forty-seven minutes till the train goes! You must go off to the station in twenty minutes. Hurry up. (4.10)

Thought: Lopakhin keeps time in the play, from beginning to end. It's clear that his modern and efficient way of doing things has triumphed over Lubov's romantic and elliptical way.

Wealth Quotes

ANYA. She's already sold her villa near Mentone; she's nothing left, nothing. And I haven't a copeck left either; we only just managed to get here. And mother won't understand! We had dinner at a station; she asked for all the expensive things, and tipped the waiters one rouble each. And Charlotta too. Yasha wants his share too--it's too bad. Mother's got a footman now, Yasha; we've brought him here. (1.50)

Thought: Though she was raised by Lubov, Anya doesn't have the attachment to luxury she criticizes here. Perhaps, like Varya, she's always lived with anxiety about money.

GAEV. My sister hasn't lost the habit of throwing money about. (1.189)

Thought: Like Lubov, Gaev accepts flagrancy with money as part of his birthright. He notices that his sister wastes a lot of money, but certainly makes no move to stop her.

LUBOV. [Looks in her purse] I had a lot of money yesterday, but there's very little to-day. My poor Varya feeds everybody on milk soup to save money, in the kitchen the old people only get peas, and I spend recklessly. [Drops the purse, scattering gold coins] There, they are all over the place. (2.29)

Thought: Dropping the gold coins gives us a visual symbol of Lubov's recklessness with money. She recognizes her problem, but does nothing to change her behavior.

PISCHIK. But the trouble is, I've no money! A hungry dog only believes in meat. [Snores and wakes up again immediately] So I ...only believe in money. (3.1)

Thought: Pischik is the comic foil to Ranevskaya and Gaev. Like them, he's a landowner in need of cash to pay his mortgage, but Chekhov writes him as a buffoon. In the end, Pischik gives in to development by allowing a company to drill on his land.

TROFIMOV. [To PISCHIK] If the energy which you, in the course of your life, have spent in looking for money to pay interest had been used for something else, then, I believe, after all, you'd be able to turn everything upside down. (3.9)

Thought: While Lubov and Gaev spend little time trying to solve their problem, Pischik is constantly running around looking for money. He's rewarded at the end of the play by the discovery of natural resources on his land.

TROFIMOV. I think, Ermolai Alexeyevitch, that you're a rich man, and you'll soon be a millionaire. Just as the wild beast which eats everything it finds is needed for changes to take place in matter, so you are needed too. (3.95)

Thought: Trofimov looks at most things and people (except for Anya) from a scientific perspective. He regards Lopakhin's wealth as a necessary force of nature.

LOPAKHIN. You know, I get up at five every morning, I work from morning till evening, I am always dealing with money--my own and other people's--and I see what people are like. You've only got to begin to do anything to find out how few honest, honourable people there are. (3.106)

LOPAKHIN. In the spring I sowed three thousand acres of poppies, and now I've made forty thousand roubles net profit. And when my poppies were in flower, what a picture it was! So I, as I was saying, made forty thousand roubles, and I mean I'd like to lend you some, because I can afford it. Why turn up your nose at it? I'm just a simple peasant. (4.28)

Thought: We wonder why Lopakhin is so adamant about offering money? Does he truly want to help Trofimov? Does he want some power over him? As Lubov has rejected his help, is he searching for a way to feel useful?

TROFIMOV. Even if you gave me twenty thousand I should refuse. I'm a free man. And everything that all you people, rich and poor, value so highly and so dearly hasn't the least influence over me; it's like a flock of down in the wind. (4.29)

Thought: Trofimov claims to be above love and above money. We don't really believe his claims about love – he's obviously smitten with Anya – but he does seem genuinely indifferent to money. What do you think?

GAEV. I'm a bank official now, and a financier (4.55)

Thought: Gaev is going to try working for a living, and seems to derive some pleasure from anticipating how industrious he'll be. Lopakhin believes Gaev will give up.

Contrasting Regions Quotes

ANYA. We went to Paris; it's cold there and snowing. I talk French perfectly horribly. My mother lives on the fifth floor. I go to her, and find her there with various Frenchmen, women, an old abbé with a book, and everything in tobacco smoke and with no comfort at all. (1.48)

Thought: Anya reacts negatively to the foreignness of Paris: the living quarters, the language, the people, the religion, and the habits. She wants to save her mother from this alien world.

LUBOV. But suppose I'm dreaming! God knows I love my own country, I love it deeply; I couldn't look out of the railway carriage, I cried so much. (1.96)

Thought: Lubov's overwhelming emotional response upon returning home creates high stakes for the loss of that home. It also increases our frustration when Lubov does nothing to save it.

LUBOV. Last year, when they had sold the villa to pay my debts, I went away to Paris, and there he robbed me of all I had and threw me over and went off with another woman. I tried to poison myself. ... It was so silly, so shameful. ... And suddenly I longed to be back in Russia, my own land, with my little girl. (1.59)

Thought: For Lubov, escaping to Russia becomes the solution to the problems in Paris. When the problems in Russia become insurmountable, she'll return to Paris.

DUNYASHA. I hardly knew you, Yasha. You have changed abroad. (1.66)

Thought: Dunyasha is attracted to Yasha's new cosmopolitan airs. Her crush seems to stem from a combination of sexual interest and a belief that he might be a key to upward mobility.

PISCHIK. [To LUBOV ANDREYEVNA] What about Paris? Eh? Did you eat frogs?

LUBOV. I ate crocodiles. (1.120)

Thought: Lubov's stay in Paris gives her an exoticism that excites the men at home.

VARYA. There are two telegrams for you, little mother. [Picks out a key and noisily unlocks an antique cupboard] Here they are.

LUBOV. They're from Paris. ... [Tears them up without reading them] I've done with Paris. (1.125)

Thought: In a wily use of a prop – the telegram – Chekhov gives us a visual representation of Lubov's changing attitude toward home and Paris. In Act 1, she tears the telegrams up without reading them. By Act 3, she's hiding them in her sleeve.

CHARLOTTA. [Thoughtfully] I haven't a real passport. (2.1)

Thought: Charlotta's the only character without a strong allegiance to Paris or Russia. Her independence frees her from the painful attachments of, say, Lubov, but it doesn't seem to fulfill her.

DUNYASHA. [To YASHA] Still, it must be nice to live abroad.

YASHA. Yes, certainly. I cannot differ from you there. [Yawns and lights a cigar.]

EPIKHODOV. That is perfectly natural. Abroad everything is in full complexity. (2.6-8)

Thought: Epikhodov tries to sound educated and knowledgeable to compete with Yasha. Instead, he makes strange pronouncements like this.

YASHA. If you go to Paris again, then please take me with you. It's absolutely impossible for me to stop here. [Looking round; in an undertone] What's the good of talking about it, you see for yourself that this is an uneducated country, with an immoral population, and it's so dull. (3.92)

Thought: Yasha has none of the sentimental attachment to Russia shared by Lubov, Gaev, and Anya. He wants excitement and escape. He also wants to sever ties with his peasant past, in the shape of his mother.

YASHA. What's the use of crying? [Drinks champagne] In six days I'll be again in Paris. To-morrow we get into the express and off we go. I can hardly believe it. Vive la France! It doesn't suit me here, I can't live here … it's no good. Well, I've seen the uncivilized world; I have had enough of it. [Drinks champagne] (4.49)

Thought: Though they come from the same place, Yasha uses his travel as an excuse to discard Dunyasha as something lower than he.

Plot Analysis

Classic Plot Analysis

Initial Situation
Lubov and Gaev return to their childhood home on the cherry orchard.
The beginning of the play establishes the deep emotional attachment Lubov and others have to the cherry orchard. At this point, it is unthinkable that the estate could be lost.

Conflict
Lopakhin announces that the cherry orchard will be sold.
Lopakhin, the pragmatist, shares his plan for the orchard: clear it and cut it up into lots. Lubov and Gaev would never consider such a thing.

Complication
Lubov and Gaev stall on making any decisions. The transient enters to remind them of the weight of the past.
In the very orchard that's the source of conflict, Lubov and Gaev simply enjoy its beauty. Lopakhin reminds them once more that the auction date is approaching and they must make a decision. Trofimov, while not a fan of Lopakhin's schemes, favors getting rid of the orchard. For him it's a symbol of injustice.

Climax

At the party, Lopakhin announces that he's bought the orchard.

While trying to entertain, Lubov waits in agony for the men to return from the auction. Drumroll: Lopakhin bought it! He gives a big, dramatic speech in which the purchase of the orchard emerges almost as an act of revenge for his ancestor's servitude.

Suspense

What will they do next?

There's just a brief moment at the end of Act 3 – after Lopakhin has gloated and gone – when Lubov sits crying. Anya approaches her gently, reminding her that she still has her life to live. Will Lubov go somewhere new? Will she return to Paris?

Denouement

The family is moving out.

Luggage is piled up as the family waits for the train – all of them dispersing to various locations. Lopakhin excitedly starts the clearing of the orchard.

Conclusion

The family is gone. The house is locked. Fiers is left behind.

It's the end of an era, and the era's last representative, Fiers, is left alone and dying.

Booker's Seven Basic Plots Analysis: Comedy or Tragedy

Chekhov called his play a "Comedy in Four Acts," provoking a famous argument with the director Stanislavsky (see "Genre"). What about the ending: the tearful eviction, the dying old man? It's sad! Can we break with Chekhov and call it a tragedy? Does it depend on who we name the protagonist (see "Character Roles")? Let's try it both ways.

Comedy: Shadow of Confusion

The family returns to the estate.

Lubov, Gaev, Varya, and Anya are all confused about how to take action to save the cherry orchard. Lopakhin suggests leasing the land for summer estates, but they deny him. No one in the family sees a clear way forward.

Comedy: Nightmarish Tangle

Lubov and Gaev refuse to come up with a plan.

Everyone's in a state of conflict at the picnic. Lubov blames Gaev for wasting money; Dunyasha's throwing herself away on Yasha; everyone teases Varya about Lopakhin; Lopakhin threatens to leave if they don't decide something about the cherry orchard. At the party, the servants upset Varya by drinking and playing pool; Pischik loses his money; Lubov and Trofimov argue. It's all a mess.

Comedy: Coming to Light

Lopakhin buys the orchard. The family clears out.

No more uncertainty. Lopakhin is triumphant. Gaev and Lubov are forced to relinquish the past. Trofimov and Anya embark on a union, released into a future they can choose for themselves.

Tragedy: Anticipation Stage

Lubov returns home.

Lubov resolutely leaves Paris behind and wants to make being home "work," despite financial difficulties and the looming memories of death.

Tragedy: Dream Stage

No suitable solution presents itself.

If Lubov is the protagonist, she's an inactive one. Her efforts to save the cherry orchard (mostly repeating "I'm sure we'll think of something") make Gaev's look heroic.

Tragedy: Frustration Stage

Lubov begins to see the orchard slipping away.

Lubov irritably blames herself and Gaev for running the estate into the ground, and clings to Lopakhin in the hopes that he'll come up with a plan they can accept. At the party, she attacks Trofimov. The idea of Paris – and her sick lover – seem to sound better and better.

Tragedy: Nightmare Stage

Lubov discovers that the orchard now belongs to Lopakhin.

Lopakhin bought the orchard, and she knows what he'll do with it. The house, the nursery she loved, the orchard – they'll all be torn down.

Tragedy: Destruction or Death Wish Stage

Lubov leaves the orchard.

While she struggles to present a brave front, a moment alone with Gaev reveals her Lubov's true feelings. She is shattered to leave the orchard.

Three Act Plot Analysis

Yes, you're right: Chekhov wrote his play in four acts, not three. This Three Act Plot Analysis is just another way of breaking up the text to understand the way it works. With the meandering structure of Chekhov's plays, we need all the help we can get.

Act I

While there are a number of story lines in the play, the main story question is, "will the cherry orchard be saved?" So "Act I" in this case does seem to encompass Chekhov's Act I, when the orchard's nostalgic value is made clear and Lopakhin introduces the challenge of finding an alternative to the impending sale.

Act II

In "Act II," which includes Chekhov's Act II and most of Act III, we watch as Lubov and Gaev do absolutely nothing substantial toward achieving their goal (saving the orchard). Lopakhin keeps encouraging them to make a decision, but they refuse. At the end of this "Act," Lopakhin reveals that he's bought the orchard.

Act III

The family vacates the house, and Lopakhin starts building.

Study Questions

1. Does Chekhov's meandering structure support the themes he's trying to express? Detract from them?
2. If you had to side with the philosophies of Lubov, Lopakhin, or Trofimov, which would it be?
3. Do you think this play punishes Lubov and Gaev for living high on the labor of serfs? How might audience members of different backgrounds view this play differently?
4. Which character(s) do you think presents Chekhov's perspective?
5. Can you think of contemporary situations that have conflicts similar to those in *The Cherry Orchard*?
6. What do you think: is *The Cherry Orchard* a comedy or a tragedy? If you were directing the play, how would you make your choice clear?

Characters

All Characters

Lubov Andreyevna Ranevskaya Character Analysis

Lubov and Money

In Act 2, Lopakhin says of Lubov and her brother, "I've never met such frivolous people as you before, or anybody so unbusinesslike and peculiar" (2.44). He has a point. Chekhov shows Lubov throwing her money away so many times it's almost overkill. She loans money to Pischik in Act 1. She overtips the waiters in Act 2, then gives a homeless man a gold piece. Act 4 opens with Gaev chiding her for giving the peasants her whole purse. Why, Lubov, why?

Well, here are a few reasons. Money is not a precious thing to Lubov. She doesn't work for her money and perhaps has never truly understood that it's not an inexhaustible resource. Chekhov (who, let's remember, had two jobs) is critiquing the idleness of Russian aristocrats who, at the time he was writing, were meeting their economic comeuppance.

The critique is tempered, however, by the fact of Lubov's deeply generous nature. When she's presented with a human face asking her for help, she freely gives it. This nurturing quality is

central to her character. As Lopakhin recalls:

She's a good sort--an easy, simple person. I remember when I was a boy of fifteen, my father, who is dead--he used to keep a shop in the village here--hit me on the face with his fist, and my nose bled. ...We had gone into the yard together for something or other, and he was a little drunk. Lubov Andreyevna, as I remember her now, was still young, and very thin, and she took me to the washstand here in this very room, the nursery. She said, "Don't cry, little man, it'll be all right in time for your wedding." (1.5)

Lopakhin remembers this moment of kindness for the rest of his life.

Lubov and Love
Lubov lives for love. It's in the way she moves, as Gaev says. It influences all her actions, including her way with money, as we discussed above. She freely gives money to everyone from the homeless to her worthless lover in Paris. In Act 3, Lubov confesses to Trofimov that she wants to return to her love. Trofimov is outraged. How can she return to someone who robbed her blind? She doesn't care about that. He needs her:

LUBOV. That wild man is ill again, he's bad again. ... He begs for forgiveness, and implores me to come, and I really ought to go to Paris to be near him. You look severe, Peter, but what can I do, my dear, what can I do; he's ill, he's alone, unhappy, and who's to look after him, who's to keep him away from his errors, to give him his medicine punctually? And why should I conceal it and say nothing about it; I love him, that's plain, I love him, I love him. ...That love is a stone round my neck; I'm going with it to the bottom, but I love that stone and can't live without it. (3.60)

Human connections define and motivate Lubov, and she encourages them in others: in Anya and Trofimov, Varya and Lopakhin. Her emotional nature drives her decisions, and is part of what makes it impossible for her to let go of the past.

Lubov and the Past
It breaks our heart when Lubov sees her mother in the orchard. She's in the nursery, willing herself back in time:

LUBOV. [Looks out into the garden] Oh, my childhood, days of my innocence! In this nursery I used to sleep; I used to look out from here into the orchard. Happiness used to wake with me every morning, and then it was just as it is now; nothing has changed.

Suddenly a tree branch shape-shifts into a woman in white, Lubov's mother. Lubov holds the impossible hope that returning home can make her a child again. She'd like to wipe out everything shameful and unpleasant in her adult life. To start over. In some ways, as Lubov gives up the orchard and acknowledges the present, we're watching her grow up again.

Lubov Andreyevna Ranevskaya Timeline and Summary

- Lubov returns to her childhood home in Russia after five years in Paris. She was involved there with a man who bled her dry financially, then cheated on her.
- She learns from Lopakhin that the estate will be sold in three months. She and her brother Gaev reject Lopakhin's suggestion of turning the orchard into vacation lots.
- Lubov sees Trofimov, her son's old tutor, and is reminded of Grisha's death.
- In the second act, Lubov still refuses to come up with a plan for the estate. She continues to spend money unwisely.
- The third act finds Lubov waiting anxiously for the result of the auction. Gaev's been sent with far too little money.
- She learns that Lopakhin has bought the estate. She is crushed.
- In Act 4, Lubov is leaving home again, with the intention of returning to her lover in Paris.

Ermolai Lopakhin Character Analysis

Lopakhin the Peasant

Lopakhin is the son of a former serf (essentially a slave) who worked on Lubov's estate. He was a drunk and ignorant man who beat Lopakhin. Like his father, Lopakhin isn't an educated man, and admits as much: "Here I've been reading this book, but I understood nothing. I read and fell asleep" (1.5). Both Lubov and Gaev make references to Lopakhin's lack of refinement, and it's one of the reasons they don't listen to him. In their opinion, as a former peasant, Lopakhin surely can't appreciate the value of the orchard's beauty – he wants to cut it down, for goodness' sake.

LUBOV. Cut it down? My dear man, you must excuse me, but you don't understand anything at all. If there's anything interesting or remarkable in the whole province, it's this cherry orchard of ours. (1.111)

And it's true, Lopakhin can be tactless and oblivious. At the end of the play he shows extreme insensitivity in cutting down the cherry trees before Lubov has even left. But Chekhov didn't write a caveman. Lopakhin has the hands of an artist, remarks Trofimov, and he recognizes beauty. He just can't afford to place beauty over everything else. He tells Trofimov:

LOPAKHIN. In the spring I sowed three thousand acres of poppies, and now I've made forty thousand roubles net profit. And when my poppies were in flower, what a picture it was! So I, as I was saying, made forty thousand roubles, and I mean I'd like to lend you some, because I can afford it. Why turn up your nose at it? I'm just a simple peasant. .. .(4.28)

In the middle of a conversation about money, Lopakhin has a moment of reverie in the beauty of the poppies. Then it's back to business.

The Big Monologue

In a play that's sparing with show-stopping moments, Lopakhin's Big Monologue stands out. He returns from the auction, a little drunk, and announces that he's bought the orchard. The music screeches to a stop. What begins as a careful retelling of the auction's progress morphs into a cathartic confession of Lopakhin's deepest motives. Lubov's pain is far from his mind as he exults:

The cherry orchard is mine now, mine! [Roars with laughter] My God, my God, the cherry orchard's mine! Tell me I'm drunk, or mad, or dreaming. ... [Stamps his feet] Don't laugh at me! If my father and grandfather rose from their graves and looked at the whole affair, and saw how their Ermolai, their beaten and uneducated Ermolai, who used to run barefoot in the winter, how that very Ermolai has bought an estate, which is the most beautiful thing in the world! I've bought the estate where my grandfather and my father were slaves, where they weren't even allowed into the kitchen. (3.151)

The speech is a fascinating dramatic moment. Lopakhin's joy and release is so big and ugly we want to look away even as we applaud the justice of his act. We feel bad for Lubov – but doesn't she kind of deserve to hear it? In its contradictions and divided allegiances, this moment is pure Chekhov.

Why Doesn't He Marry Varya!?

It's a topic of conversation from Act 1 straight through Act 4. Varya wants to marry Lopakhin, though her motives may be questionable. And Lopakhin never seems exactly *against* the idea. So why, when Lubov gives him a final prod, does he sit with Varya in silence, talk about the weather, then scram gratefully when someone calls his name? We've turned this one over in our minds a lot, and considered the following explanations:

1. He just doesn't want to get married at all.
2. He's actually in love with Lubov.
3. He wants to focus on his business. (Varya consoles herself with this one.)
4. To truly escape his peasant past, he must break all ties with it. He cuts down the orchard where his father was a serf; he tears down the house. How could he possibly marry into the family that enslaved his?
5. All of the above.

What do you think?

Ermolai Lopakhin Timeline and Summary

- Lopakhin welcomes Lubov, who's just returned from Paris. He reminds her that the estate auction has been set for August 22nd, and suggests a plan to save the estate. Lubov is not interested.
- In Act 2, Lopakhin urges Lubov and Gaev to take action, but they decline. He gets

frustrated.
- Lopakhin buys the orchard. He plans to turn it into vacation homes right away.
- Lopakhin sees off Lubov and the family. He does not propose to Varya.

Trofimov Character Analysis

Trofimov the Revolutionary

When Trofimov speaks, it's hard not hear the voice of Chekhov. He talks about work: "everything that is unattainable now will some day be near at hand and comprehensible, but we must work" (2.105). He's concerned with human health: "the vast majority of us…live like savages, fighting and cursing at the slightest opportunity, eating filthily, sleeping in the dirt, in stuffiness, with fleas, stinks, smells, moral filth" (2.105). He's idealistic: "My soul is always my own; every minute of the day and the night it is filled with unspeakable presentiments. I know that happiness is coming, Anya, I see it already" (2.153). He is the revolutionary obsessed with the future, while those around him are trapped in the past. Anya is his follower, and he makes her understand the wider sociopolitical impact of her family's history:

Think, Anya, your grandfather, your great-grandfather, and all your ancestors were serf-owners, they owned living souls; and now, doesn't something human look at you from every cherry in the orchard, every leaf and every stalk? (2.149)

As an outsider, Trofimov brings an objective viewpoint to the situation. He doesn't side with Lubov or Lopakhin when it comes to the cherry orchard. When asked what he thinks of Lopakhin, Trofimov replies:

TROFIMOV. I think, Ermolai Alexeyevitch, that you're a rich man, and you'll soon be a millionaire. Just as the wild beast which eats everything it finds is needed for changes to take place in matter, so you are needed too. (2.95)

Trofimov likes the businessman, despite his materialism, and engages Lopakhin as an equal (which is more than Lubov and Gaev do).

Trofimov the Eternal Student

Trofimov is intelligent and impassioned, but he's also immature. There's a reason Chekhov calls him the Eternal Student. He's judgmental and unforgiving, and Lubov blames it on his youth:

You boldly look forward, isn't it because you cannot foresee or expect anything terrible, because so far life has been hidden from your young eyes? You are bolder, more honest, deeper than we are, but think only, be just a little magnanimous, and have mercy on me. (3.65)

Trofimov lacks real world experience and lacks Lubov's emotional intelligence, her power to

empathize with others' pain. His pigheadedness earns him some ridicule. After Lubov's scathing assessment at the party (her only moment of open cruelty) he falls down the stairs.

Leonid Andreyevich Gaev Character Analysis

Gaev the Big Baby

Lopakhin calls Gaev an old woman, but we think Gaev is more like a big baby. He loves candy, plays air-pool, and still can't dress himself. Fiers continually worries over his choice of clothing: "[Brushing GAEV'S trousers; in an insistent tone] You've put on the wrong trousers again. What am I to do with you?" (1.159). The small details hint at Gaev's immaturity. He's been spoiled and babied all his life; there's no way he's up to the challenge he and Lubov now face. He tells Varya:

I work my brains to their hardest. I've several remedies, very many, and that really means I've none at all. It would be nice to inherit a fortune from somebody, it would be nice to marry our Anya to a rich man, it would be nice to go to Yaroslav and try my luck with my aunt the Countess. (1.197)

These strokes of luck are the only options Gaev can imagine. The idea of working himself does not occur to him yet.

Gaev's Speeches

Gaev is notorious for lecturing at length, at any and all times, on any and all subjects. First we are subjected to an ode to a bookcase:

GAEV. My dear and honored case! I congratulate you on your existence, which has already for more than a hundred years been directed towards the bright ideals of good and justice; your silent call to productive labor has not grown less in the hundred years [Weeping] during which you have upheld virtue and faith in a better future to the generations of our race, educating us up to ideals of goodness and to the knowledge of a common consciousness. [Pause.] (1.129)

Why on earth would Chekhov have Gaev make a speech to a bookcase, except to make him look like a numbskull? It's about context. Perhaps Gaev is thinking of the changes the bookcase – and by extension, the house – has seen in the last hundred years. Remember, Lopakhin has just reminded them that the orchard will be sold. Perhaps Gaev is thinking, all this will be gone soon. When the sun sets in Act 2, Gaev declaims:

O Nature, thou art wonderful, thou shinest with eternal radiance! Oh, beautiful and indifferent one, thou whom we call mother, thou containest in thyself existence and death, thou livest and destroyest. (2.111)

Everyone groans and tells him to zip it. He's just silly Uncle Leon. But in reality, what he says has a bearing on their situation. The beauty of their land, soon to be littered with vacation

homes, catches him. Gaev acknowledges the indifference of nature and accepts that "all things must come to an end" – including, the life of the house and his own life.

Master Gaev

Gaev considers himself a generous benefactor of the peasants:

I can still say that I've suffered for my beliefs. The peasants don't love me for nothing, I assure you. We've got to learn to know the peasants! We ought to learn how. ... (1.214)

But the reality is that he's deeply uncomfortable with them. When the Passerby enters the scene in Act 2, Gaev freezes, letting Lubov give away money she can't afford to lose. Only once the man has exited does Gaev speak: "My hands are all trembling; I haven't played billiards for a long time" (2.139).

Gaev prefers peasants who fit into a familiar mode from the past, like Fiers. Upwardly mobile peasants irritate him, and he rarely misses an opportunity to put both Yasha and Lopakhin "in their places," usually with a comic reference to what they smell like. When Lopakhin makes small talk in Act 1, Gaev responds, "It smells of patchouli (cheap cologne) here" (1.86). And in the departure scene in Act 4, Gaev is quick to observe, glancing at Yasha, that "somebody smells of herring!" (4.52). Things in Russia are changing too fast for Gaev.

Anya Character Analysis

Everyone in the play is a little obsessed with Lubov's seventeen-year-old daughter Anya. Dunyasha calls her "darling" and "pet" (1.32), and Varya calls her "darling" and "pretty one" (1.43). Gaev gets a little crazy telling her good night: "My darling! [Kisses ANYA'S face and hands] My child. ... [Crying] You're not my niece, you're my angel, you're my all" (1.204). And when Trofimov sees her at the end of Act 1, he whispers, "My sun! My spring!" (1.223). Anya, Anya, Anya. What's so special about her?

As befitting the Eternal Student, Trofimov has hit it on the head. She's Spring. She's what the older generation wishes they still were: a child. All of her life choices are ahead of her, not in a past to be regretted.

A surprisingly minor and inactive character, Anya does undergo one important change in the play. In Act 1, she shares her mother's viewpoint entirely. She loves home and agonizes with Varya over the fate of the orchard:

ANYA. Oh God, oh God ...
VARYA. The place will be sold in August.
ANYA. O God. ... (1.54-56)

At the end of Act 2, her romance with Trofimov has changed her:

What have you done to me, Peter? I don't love the cherry orchard as I used to. I loved it so

tenderly, I thought there was no better place in the world than our orchard. (2.148)

She promises to leave the estate. When the orchard is sold, Anya, sensitive and caring like her mother, comforts Lubov: "don't cry mother, you've still got your life before you, you've still your beautiful pure soul" (3.134). But her relief is apparent as they leave. Even Lubov notices it through her grief:

LUBOV. [Passionately kisses her daughter] My treasure, you're radiant, your eyes flash like two jewels! Are you happy? Very?

ANYA. Very! A new life is beginning, mother! (4.53-54)

Young and full of curiosity, Anya wants to read and study. She's still able to change her mind and her ways. She embodies hope.

Varya Character Analysis

We don't know about you, but if we had to choose to be someone in this play, it wouldn't be Varya. She has it hard. Nobody calls her "darling" or "pretty one" like they do Anya. Lubov, her own (adopted) mother observes, "Varya is just as she used to be, just like a nun" (1.26). Always jangling her caretaker's keychain, she's uptight, conservative, a bit bossy. When Lubov returns, Varya tries to keep Trofimov away and runs everybody off: "Well, sirs, it's getting on for three, quite time you went" (1.93).

Varya's not a laugh, but how could she be? She carries the responsibility of the entire estate. When Lubov wastes money on elaborate lunches, does Lubov face the starving peasants? Nope. It's Varya. No wonder she wants to escape to a convent. Her encounters with the world have been less than inspiring.

Is she in love with Lopakhin? Who knows? She's lonely. She's a practical woman and she respects him. He works as hard as she does and knows the value of a buck. But, as she says, she can't propose to him herself.

Fiers Character Analysis

Chekhov describes Fiers's first entrance like so: "leaning on a stick, [he] walks quickly across the stage; he has just been to meet Lubov Andreyevna. He wears an old-fashioned livery and a tall hat" (1.24). We immediately know 1) he's old, 2) he's old-fashioned, and 3) he hops to it when his mistress needs something. Fiers is 87 years old and thinks things were better before the serfs were freed: "When the Emancipation came I was already first valet. Only I didn't agree with the Emancipation and remained with my people. ... [Pause] I remember everybody was happy, but they didn't know why" (2.79).

Fiers is deaf and senile. This perfectly natural character detail enables Chekhov to repeatedly

conjure up old Russia:

FIERS. In the old days, forty or fifty years back, they dried the cherries, soaked them and pickled them, and made jam of them, and it used to happen that...

GAEV. Be quiet, Fiers.

FIERS. And then we'd send the dried cherries off in carts to Moscow and Kharkov. And money! And the dried cherries were soft, juicy, sweet, and nicely scented...They knew the way....

LUBOV. What was the way?

FIERS. They've forgotten. Nobody remembers . (1.115-119)

With his memories, his loyalty to the family, the way he looks and behaves, Fiers stokes the fire of Lubov and Gaev's attachment to the cherry orchard. He evokes the past. But with the estate in decline, Fiers becomes a problem to solve. In Act 4, Lubov has "two anxieties [...]. The first is poor Fiers [Looks at her watch]. We've still five minutes." (4.74). Anya assures her that Yasha has taken care of Fiers. They've left the fate of the faithful old servant in the hands of the faithless young one. We can guess what happens, but the ending of the play still shocks us. Fiers tries the handle to the door:

FIERS. It's locked. They've gone away. [Sits on a sofa] They've forgotten about me. ... Never mind, I'll sit here. ... And Leonid Andreyevitch will have gone in a light overcoat instead of putting on his fur coat. ... [Sighs anxiously] I didn't see. ... Oh, these young people! [Mumbles something that cannot be understood] Life's gone on as if I'd never lived. [Lying down] I'll lie down. ... You've no strength left in you, nothing left at all. ... Oh, you ...bungler!

[He lies without moving.] (1.134)

With the necessity of forward movement pressing on them, the family has forgotten Fiers. They abandon him, a relic of the past.

Boris Semyonov-Pischik Character Analysis

Pischik, Lubov's landowning neighbor, provides some context for the struggles of Lubov's family. Pischik's constant search for money lets us know that the whole community of landowners faces the same financial straits. Unlike Lubov, however, Pischik is entirely comic. He's always doing ridiculous things like swallowing all of Lubov's pills or comparing himself to a horse. Every time he comes over, he begs for money, even the first night Lubov is back in town:

PISCHIK. [Follows her] Yes, we've got to go to bed. ... Oh, my gout! I'll stay the night here. If only, Lubov Andreyevna, my dear, you could get me 240 roubles to-morrow morning--

GAEV. Still the same story…

PISCHIK. Two hundred and forty roubles ... to pay the interest on the mortgage.

LUBOV. I haven't any money, dear man.

PISCHIK. I'll give it back ... it's a small sum. ...

LUBOV. Well, then, Leonid will give it to you. ... Let him have it, Leonid.

GAEV. By all means; hold out your hand.

LUBOV. Why not? He wants it; he'll give it back . (1.181-182)

In the end, Pischik surprises everyone by paying back these little loans. Some Englishmen found clay on his land and he's leased it to them. While Lubov and Gaev sneer at the idea of vacation homes in their cherry orchard, Pischik's not too proud. His adaptability allows him to keep his estate.

Semyon Epikhodov Character Analysis

Epikhodov offers pretty much straight comic relief from his first entrance in Act 1, when he "enters with a bouquet. He wears a short jacket and brilliantly polished boots which squeak audibly. He drops the bouquet as he enters, then picks it up" (1.10). As an accountant for an estate with no money, his very presence is kind of a joke. And he's a consistent source of slapstick humor and malapropisms (words made up or used incorrectly). As Dunyasha notes early on, "he's a nice young man, but every now and again, when he begins talking, you can't understand a word he's saying…He's an unlucky man; every day something happens. We tease him about it. They call him 'Two-and-twenty troubles'" (1.18).

Epikhodov's a clown, sure, but he also serves a deeper purpose in the play. In his unrequited love for Dunyasha, he's an unfortunate victim of the "upward mobility fever" infecting the younger working-class characters. Yasha's travels and gentlemanly pose attract Dunyasha, who fancies herself a quasi-lady. Epikhodov seems beneath her now. He works hard to regain her attentions and mostly fails:

EPIKHODOV. I'm an educated man, I read various remarkable books, but I cannot understand the direction I myself want to go—whether to live or to shoot myself, as it were. So, in case, I always carry a revolver about with me. Here it is. [Shows a revolver.] (2.10)

There's something both amusing and sad about his pathetic attempts to win Dunyasha. To look cool, he apes Yasha's impertinence in Act 3. He plays billiards, breaks a cue, and defies his boss, Varya. Everything turns out OK for Epikhodov, however. When Lopakhin buys the estate, he leaves Epikhodov in charge:

LOPAKHIN. Yes, all, I think. [To EPIKHODOV, putting on his coat] You see that everything's quite straight, Epikhodov.
EPIKHODOV. [Hoarsely] You may depend upon me, Ermolai Alexeyevitch!
LOPAKHIN. What's the matter with your voice?
EPIKHODOV. I swallowed something just now; I was having a drink of water. (4.108-109)

What is Lopakhin thinking? Perhaps it's Chekhov's final comment on the age of gracelessness descending on the estate.

Dunyasha Character Analysis

Oh, Dunyasha. What a classic story, huh? Maid Runs Afoul of Dashing Young Rogue. And Yasha isn't even a nobleman – he's a servant posing as a nobleman.

Next to Yasha, Dunyasha probably has the least redeeming traits of any character in the play. She's vain, self-absorbed, and silly about romance. Before Yasha enters the picture, she's telling everyone about Epikhodov's crush on her. To the uninterested Lopakhin, she shares, "I may confess to you, Ermolai Alexeyevitch, that Epikhodov has proposed to me" (1.16), and five minutes later informs exhausted Anya:

DUNYASHA. I must tell you at once, I can't bear to wait a minute.

ANYA. [Tired] Something else now ...?

DUNYASHA. The clerk, Epikhodov, proposed to me after Easter.

ANYA. Always the same. ... (1.32-35)

What Epikhodov doesn't have is status. Dunyasha wants hers raised. She keeps her hands white (i.e., stays away from physical labor) and does her hair like a lady, attracting a reprimand from Lopakhin. When Yasha appears – arrogant, yawning, and probably all dressed up – he seems to be an answer to her prayers. He squeezes her once, calls her cucumber (ick), and she's a goner. In Act 2, she confesses:

DUNYASHA. I'm awfully in love with you; you're educated, you can talk about everything. [Pause.]
YASHA. [Yawns] Yes. (2.20-21)

Of course it ends in heartbreak. Lubov decides to return to Paris – pursuing her own good-for-nothing crush – and Yasha will go with her. Dunyasha hugs Yasha and cries:

DUNYASHA. [Looks in a small mirror and powders her face] Send me a letter from Paris. You know I loved you, Yasha, so much! I'm a sensitive creature, Yasha . (4.50)

Just like her mistress, Dunyasha holds on to her illusions.

Yasha Character Analysis

In a play that meticulously strives to show both the good and bad in people, Yasha is pretty much all bad. He's so unlikable that we wonder if Chekhov was working out some sort of grudge. An opportunistic parasite, Yasha weasels his way into Lubov's favor; she seems to have a soft spot for less-than-upstanding men. Yasha's not in the house five minutes before he preys on Dunyasha:

DUNYASHA. *When you went away I was only so high. [Showing with her hand] I'm Dunyasha, the daughter of Theodore Kozoyedov. You don't remember!*

YASHA. *Oh, you little cucumber!*

[Looks round and embraces her. She screams and drops a saucer. YASHA goes out quickly.] (1.68-69)

She falls for him, though it's clear he's using her:

YASHA. *[Yawns] Yes. I think this: if a girl loves anybody, then that means she's immoral…Somebody's coming. It's the mistress, and people with her. [DUNYASHA embraces him suddenly] Go to the house, as if you'd been bathing in the river; go by this path, or they'll meet you and will think I've been meeting you. I can't stand that sort of thing* . (2.21)

He's happy to make out with her, call her cucumber (weird), and give her lessons on how to stay in her place. He's not so happy being seen with her or jeopardizing his job.

Yasha's also unhappy remembering that he has a mother. When he first arrives, he refuses to see her, and when he departs in Act 4, he complains, "She'll make me lose all patience!" (4.47). His mother is a reminder of his peasant past – the last thing he wants to think about. He can't wait to get on that train to Paris.

Have you noticed that he yawns all the time, too? He acts like he's just above it all, including Russia. After taking pains to point out the Lopakhin's champagne isn't the real stuff, he guzzles it:

YASHA. *What's the use of crying? [Drinks champagne] In six days I'll be again in Paris. To-morrow we get into the express and off we go. I can hardly believe it. Vive la France! It doesn't suit me here, I can't live here ... it's no good. Well, I've seen the uncivilized world; I have had enough of it. [Drinks champagne]* (4.49)

Yasha's unappealing character – his pretension, his dislike of work, his freeloading – seems to be a result of a new class structure in Russia sorting itself out. As Fiers says, before the Emancipation, "the peasants kept their distance from the masters and the masters kept their distance from the peasants, but now everything's all anyhow and you can't understand

anything" (2.81).

Charlotta Character Analysis

Charlotta really doesn't fit in. She cultivates eccentricity, traveling with a little dog and doing magic tricks so relentlessly that Anya complains. She is a single governess who teasingly resists any man's attempt to flirt with her:

LOPAKHIN. Excuse me, Charlotta Ivanovna, I haven't said "How do you do" to you yet. [Tries to kiss her hand.]

CHARLOTTA. [Takes her hand away] If you let people kiss your hand, then they'll want your elbow, then your shoulder, and then... (1.143-144)

She is an orphan. Her parents were traveling performers, and when they died, a German lady took care of her. Charlotta is unconventional and bohemian. While she doesn't share much stage time with Trofimov, she seems to live some of his ideals: she is "free as the wind (1.151)" and nationless; she might agree that "all Russia is our orchard. The world is great and beautiful, there are many marvelous places in it" (2.149).

Chekhov gives her long speech a place of prominence, the opening of Act 2.

CHARLOTTA. And where I came from and who I am, I don't know. ... Who my parents were--perhaps they weren't married--I don't know. [Takes a cucumber out of her pocket and eats] I don't know anything. [Pause] I do want to talk, but I haven't anybody to talk to ... I haven't anybody at all . (2.1)

Charlotta has no parents, no home, no strong identification with the past – none of the associations that make giving up the orchard so excruciating for Lubov. Yet Charlotta is just as unfulfilled, if not more so. She's lonely. She doesn't have anyone or anything to love. Perhaps Chekhov presents Charlotta as the counterexample to Lubov, to remind us that having no attachments may not be ideal, either.

The Homeless Man/Passerby Character Analysis

Various translations call him various things, but the Passerby plays the same role no matter what we call him: a rude awakening for the dreamy aristocrats. The sun has set, the "breaking string" sound is heard and Fiers recalls the emancipation of the serfs. Enter the Passerby, drunk and begging for money. Varya overreacts and shrieks, Lopakhin rushes to handle the situation, and Lubov offers a gold coin. The Passerby reminds them of the reality of the land just outside their safe, comfortable estate. The interaction is a direct reflection of Trofimov's criticism of Russian intellectuals: "They philosophize, and at the same time, the vast majority of us, ninety-nine out of a hundred, live like savages... it's obvious that all our nice talk is only carried on to distract ourselves and others" (2.105).

The Stationmaster, Postmaster, and Guest Character Analysis

These uninspiring people appear at the party to the disgust of Fiers, who has retained his high standards: "I'm not well," he says. "At our balls some time back, generals and barons and admirals used to dance, and now we send for post-office clerks and the Station-master, and even they come as a favor" (3.75).

Character Roles

Protagonist
Lubov
Lubov doesn't do anything active to save the cherry orchard; she wrings her hands and waits. But she's the emotional center of the play. We feel her joy at the top of Act 1 and empathize with her grief at the end of Act 2.

Protagonist
Lopakhin
Lopakhin, on the other hand, is very active in the play. He's a source of energy in each act, and instigates the major plot upheaval, the sale of the orchard. If we believe the play is a comedy, Lopakhin is the hero. In dissolving the orchard, site of his past enslavement, he secures a happy ending.

Antagonist
Lubov or Lopakhin
If you think of Lubov as the protagonist, then Lopakhin could be seen as the antagonist. The reverse also holds true. It's true that their clashes are relatively indirect and amicable, but they are working for opposing objectives in the play and have very different ideas about what should be done with the cherry orchard.

Character Clues

Names
Readers of Chekhov sometimes complain about the Russian names. If you're not familiar with Russian names, it can be hard at first to keep up with how they change throughout the play. Here's how it works. Russians have three names:

1. A first name: Lubov
2. A patronymic name identifying one's father: Andreyevna (daughter of Andre)
3. A last name: Ranevskaya

What characters call each other tells us something about the closeness of their relationships. In

his first speeches, Lopakhin refers to Lubov as "Lubov Andreyevna," which is formal and respectful. Gaev, her brother, calls her "Luba," an affectionate nickname.

Social Status

In a play about social change, economic backgrounds go a long way in defining character. Lubov and Gaev are members of the aristocracy and, though the glory years are over and they are destitute, they continue to act like lords of the manor. "The peasants don't love me for nothing," declares Gaev to the embarrassment of Anya and Varya (1.214).

Lopakhin, an upwardly mobile member of the middle class and son of a former serf, is always slightly apologetic about his background: "I've never learned anything, my handwriting is bad, I write so that I'm quite ashamed before people, like a pig!" (2.64). The difference in class between him and Lubov does seem to be one reason she won't listen to him, as his ideas seem vulgar to her.

And the servants are in a constant (comic) class warfare with each other, as Epikhodov seeks to impress Dunyasha with his learning, she tries to impress Yasha with her white hands, and Yasha lords his worldliness over them all: "It doesn't suit me here, I can't live here ... it's no good. Well, I've seen the uncivilized world; I have had enough of it" (4.49).

Direct Characterization

It's not unusual to find a Chekhov character saying directly what he or she thinks of himself. Whether Chekhov (and the audience) agrees depends largely on the context.

Lopakhin: "I'm rich now, with lots of money, but just think about it and examine me, and you'll find I'm still a peasant down to the marrow of my bones." (1.5)

Lopakhin knows himself pretty well and owns up to his background.

Dunyasha: "I'm so tender and so delicate now; respectable and afraid of everything." (2.18)

This is Dunyasha trying to attract Yasha by boasting of her refinement. He's a servant, but she thinks of him as a gentleman.

Lubov: Then I suppose I must be beneath love. (3.54)

Like Lopakhin, Lubov sees her faults with relative clarity, though she does nothing to improve them. She's responding to Trofimov's claim that he and Anya are above love – another direct statement that, from our perspective, doesn't seem quite accurate.

Literary Devices

Symbols, Imagery, Allegory

Cherry Orchard

The beautiful white orchard means different things to different people. It represents Lubov's heritage and her youth – a disappearing paradise. For Gaev, it's a symbol of status, mentioned in the encyclopedia. For Lopakhin the cherry orchard is complicated; his attachment to Lubov makes him want to save it, while his memory of a difficult childhood urges him to destroy it. It's also a financial opportunity. Trofimov sees the orchard as a symbol of injustice, because of the way the aristocrats treated the peasants before the emancipation of the Serfs, and Anya gives up her sentimental attachment to it for a new life.

Breaking String

The breaking string sounds just before the homeless man enters in Act 2, and just after Fiers lies down at the end of the play. Different productions have handled it different ways. It could be the melancholy, nostalgic sound of a breaking guitar string. It could symbolize the discontinuation of memory. Overtly political productions have featured the sound of a snapping whip, a reminder of the family's dependence on slavery.

Setting

A provincial estate in Russia at the turn of the twentieth century

In February of 1861, Alexander II emancipated serfs in Russia. Serfs were very much like slaves, but different in that they were attached to the land. If a piece of land was sold, serfs stayed with it and served the new landowner. Before the emancipation (what Fiers calls "the disaster"), there were more than 22 million serfs in Russia, 44% of the population. This new freedom affected not only the serfs, now unemployed, but also the landowners, who couldn't thrive without the cheap labor. Rural areas were still adjusting to the shock forty years later, when Chekhov wrote *The Cherry Orchard*.

Act 1: The Nursery. May.

Setting the first scene in the nursery, Chekhov immediately establishes Lubov's intense emotional relationship with the past. Her first line is "The nursery!" Looking around, she feels like a little girl again. It's going to be very hard for her to part with this place.

Act 2: Outside, near the cherry orchard. June or July.

This act feels like a pastoral scene from Shakespeare. Love is in the air, servants tease each other, a guitar strums, and Trofimov muses on the future of man. The outdoor setting allows us to spy on interactions that could never happen in the house: the tryst between Dunyasha and Yasha, the flirtation of Trofimov and Anya, and, of course, the encounter with the homeless man. In this act, we get more closely acquainted with the beauty of the orchard, the main

subject of contention.

Act 3: The drawing room with an arch leading into the ballroom. August 22, the auction date.

How typical: Lubov throws a party while others decide the fate of the estate. The party in the ballroom serves a number of purposes. With dancing, Charlotta's magic tricks, and a few moments of slapstick, it's a theatrical contrast to the pensive mood of Act 1. It highlights the decline of the household (as Fiers mentions, "At our balls some time back, generals and barons and admirals used to dance, and now we send for post-office clerks and the Station-master, and even they come as a favour" [4.75]). It's also a last hurrah for the household, as though Lubov knows her fate is sealed.

Act 4: The Nursery. October.

The empty nursery, stripped and filled with luggage, visually represents the change that has come over the house and family since Act 1. Lubov had been so delighted, so comforted to return to the nursery, and now she's leaving it forever.

Genre

Tragicomedy

As Dolly Parton says in *Steel Magnolias* – and we may be paraphrasing here – "Laughter through tears is my favorite emotion." Chekhov felt the same, and often included stage directions suggesting a line be said while "fighting back tears," or "through tears." When Chekhov first visited rehearsals of director Stanislavsky's premiere production of *The Cherry Orchard*, however, he was appalled. The famous director had his actors weeping copiously – especially in the final act – transforming Chekhov's "Comedy in Four Acts" into a tear-jerking tragedy. Chekhov complained:

Not once does my Anya cry, nowhere do I speak of a tearful tone, in the second act there are tears in their eyes, but the tone is happy, lively. Why did you speak in your telegram about so many tears in my play? Where are they? ... Often you will find the words "through tears," but I am describing only the expression on their faces, not tears. (source: Stroud, Gregory. *Retrospective Revolution*. Urbana-Champaign, 2006. 63-4.)

Even if Chekhov's wife Olga Knipper, who played Lubov, disagreed, Chekhov insisted the play was a comedy.

Chekhov was first a writer of comic articles and popular short farces, and *The Cherry Orchard* includes a number of comic elements. Epikhodov of the squeaky boots is clearly a clown, if a sad one. Fiers's deafness provides a good amount of comic relief. Often – particularly in Act 3, when tension is highest – a character has a serious moment and is then undercut by a moment of slapstick. In an uncomfortably harsh encounter, Lubov eviscerates Trofimov for being a virgin. He runs humiliated and falls down the stairs. With this constant to-and-fro of comic and tragic elements, the play doesn't fit into a neat category. Some people have taken to calling works

like *The Cherry Orchard* "Chekhovian Comedy."

Tone

Compassionate Irony

Characterization is the center of Chekhov's work. The pivotal events of the play seem inevitable – and take place offstage. As the Chekhov translator Paul Schmidt says, Chekhov "cut[s] away the melodramatic moments of the 'plot,' or shifts them offstage, leaving finally only his characters' helpless, unheeding responses to those moments" (source: Schmidt, Paul. "Introduction." *The Plays of Anton Chekhov*. New York: Harper Perennial, 1997. p. 4).

No character in *The Cherry Orchard* is safe from Chekhov's gentle satire. With his doctor's fine powers of observation, he depicts each person's charms and weaknesses. There's not a character (except Yasha, the opportunistic parasite) with whom Chekhov doesn't seem to sympathize, so much so that when it comes to determining the protagonist, we have a few options (see "Character Roles"). Lubov is vivacious, beautiful, and generous – but she's also a self-centered and foolish, making poor decisions hurt others. We understand Lopakhin's difficult childhood as a motive for his accumulation of wealth, but boy does he make some insensitive moves. Trofimov's idealism is appealing, but his youthful arrogance isn't. He gets his comeuppance in Act 3, humiliated by the anxious Lubov. By combining virtues and flaws in each character, Chekhov achieves an affectionate distance that we in the audience share.

Writing Style

Realism

"What happens onstage should be just as complicated and just as simple as things are in real life. People are sitting at a table having dinner, that's all, but at the same time their happiness is being created, or their lives are being torn apart," wrote Chekhov of the realistic style exemplified by *The Cherry Orchard* (source). Characters wander in and out, lines of communication cross, seemingly irrelevant topics are brought up only to be dropped and taken up again later. In this deceptively scattered progression of dialogues, a complete picture of a family and society emerges.

At the end of the chaotic first act, a scene of arrival, Varya reports to her sister Anya on the maintenance of the estate:

VARYA. There's been an unpleasantness here while you were away. In the old servants' part of the house, as you know, only the old people live--little old Efim and Polya and Evstigney, and Karp as well. They started letting some tramps or other spend the night there--I said nothing. Then I heard that they were saying that I had ordered them to be fed on peas and nothing else; from meanness, you see. ... And it was all Evstigney's doing. ... Very well, I thought, if that's what the matter is, just you wait. So I call Evstigney. ... [Yawns] He comes. "What's this," I say,

"Evstigney, you old fool."... [Looks at ANYA] Anya dear! [Pause] ... My darling's gone to sleep!" (1.220)

The monologue seems like an idle, rambling complaint, but reveals a number of things about Varya, Anya, and the situation at home. We can see that, financially, things are very bad for them. The family can't afford to feed the former serfs who live on their land. And Varya responds, in her oversensitive way, by taking offense at their accusations that she's "mean" or cheap. Anya falls asleep, either unconcerned about the starving peasants or tired by Varya's pettiness.

Then the "peas" story comes up again in Act 2, when Lubov laments her flagrancy with money:

LUBOV. My poor Varya feeds everybody on milk soup to save money, in the kitchen the old people only get peas, and I spend recklessly. [Drops the purse, scattering gold coins] There, they are all over the place. (2.29)

"So it's true," we think. Varya *is* feeding them on peas. Lubov, charming as she may be, hurts more than herself with her fiscal irresponsibility, represented here by the simple, naturalistic detail of "scattering gold coins." She's also responsible for the discomfort of many others.

What's Up With the Title?

The Cherry Orchard really is about a cherry orchard. It's the central plot device in the play. The question "Will the orchard be saved?" gives us a bit of suspense in Chekhov's otherwise leisurely plotting. The cherry orchard is also the central symbol in the play; how each character responds to the orchard – and weighs in on its future – defines how they view the past. For more on that, go to "Symbolism, Imagery, Allegory."

What's Up With the Ending?

The Cherry Orchard ends with the 87-year-old servant Fiers shuffling out to find that the family has departed without him. He tries the door; it's locked. He lies down on the couch, mumbles, "Life's gone on as if I'd never lived," and grows still (4.134). Then the "breaking string" sound is heard, along with the thudding of an axe.

What to make of it? In leaving the orchard, the family finally cuts ties with the past. It will disappear from their memories, just as they've forgotten Fiers in their preparations to leave. We can't help but think, as well, that there's a last comment here on the damaging selfishness of aristocrats like Lubov and Gaev. They've already failed to take action to save the estate, and in their nostalgic, wallowing good-bye to the house, they fail to secure a safe place for their most loyal servant.

Did You Know?

Trivia

- In *Franny and Zooey*, author J.D. Salinger references *The Cherry Orchard* as an incomparably beautiful work. "You may have seen 'inspired' productions, 'competent' productions, but never anything beautiful," writes Buddy. "Never one where Chekhov's talent is matched, nuance for nuance, idiosyncrasy for idiosyncrasy, by every soul onstage." Check out *Franny and Zooey* on Shmoop to learn more. (And read the book – it's awesome.)
- A scene from *The Cherry Orchard* appears in the 2006 Robert DeNiro movie *The Good Shepherd*.
- The American short story writer Raymond Carver was deeply influenced by Chekhov. Check out this essay linking the two writers.

Steaminess Rating

PG-13
Not a lot of steaminess in *The Cherry Orchard*. Yasha and Dunyasha have a bit of a fling, but it's in PG-13 territory.

Allusions and Cultural References

Literary and Philosophical References

- Aleksey Konstantinovich Tolstoy (1817-1875), "The Magdalen" (3.72). This poem is about a woman living in sin.

Historical References

- The Emancipation of the Serfs (2.79). In 1861 Alexander II freed the serfs on private Russian estates.

Best of the Web

Websites

Chekhov Short Stories
http://chekhov2.tripod.com/
201 stories, to be precise

The Proposal
http://www.one-act-plays.com/comedies/proposal.html
Read the full text of one of Chekhov's farces, a forerunner to the comic touches in *The Cherry Orchard*.

Chekhov on the *NY Times*
http://topics.nytimes.com/topics/reference/timestopics/people/c/anton_chekhov/index.html
Chekhov's *NY Times* topic page, which provides links to all the newspaper's Chekhov-related articles

Chekhov Biography
http://people.brandeis.edu/~teuber/chekhovbio.html
Brandeis University provides a biography of Chekhov.

Movie or TV Productions

The Cherry Orchard, 1962
http://www.imdb.com/title/tt1111778/
This BBC version features Judi Dench as Anya, Peggy Ashcroft as Lubov, and John Gielgud as Gaev.

The Cherry Orchard, 1981
http://www.imdb.com/title/tt0488991/
Almost twenty years later, Judi Dench made another TV version, this time playing Lubov.

La Cerisae, 2000
http://www.imdb.com/title/tt0144134/
In this French version, Charlotte Rampling plays Lubov.

Video

The Cherry Orchard, 1962
http://www.youtube.com/watch?v=eeFMWSbincc
This 1962 production features plenty of British stars: Judi Dench as Anya, John Gielgud as Gaev, Peggy Ashcroft as Lubov. In this clip, the family returns home to the estate.

The Cherry Orchard, 1993
http://www.youtube.com/watch?v=txbdLTOOfll
A Russian version. This clip shows the party, just before Lopakhin returns with the bad news.

Anton Chekhov
http://www.youtube.com/watch?v=CY6ltl1n5Lo
A really interesting Russian montage of quotes, photos, and film clips giving a picture of
Chekhov's life.

Chekhov 101
http://www.youtube.com/watch?v=wQHovMQ8Zll&feature=fvsr
Writers from the event magazine *Time Out New York* give a humorous primer on Chekhov's
themes.

Images
The Playwright
http://www.indiana.edu/~thtr/2004/cherry_orchard/cherry_orchard_images/olga_and_anton.jpg
Chekhov and his wife, the actress Olga Knipper

Young Chekhov
http://shows.vtheatre.net/pix/chekhov01.jpg
A photo of Chekhov as a young man.

Cherry Orchard
http://www.broadwayworld.com/columnpic/Cherry%20Orchard_art.jpg
What does a cherry orchard look like, anyway?

Production Photo
http://images.nymag.com/arts/theater/reviews/cherryorchard090202_560.jpg
A picture from the 2009 production at Brooklyn Academy of Music

7364561R00032

Printed in Great Britain
by Amazon.co.uk, Ltd.,
Marston Gate.